D1456332

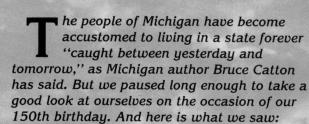

The people of Michigan have become accustomed to living in a state forever "caught between yesterday and tomorrow," as Michigan author Bruce Catton has said. But we paused long enough to take a good look at ourselves on the occasion of our 150th birthday. And here is what we saw:

A state which has had a measurable impact on America and the world in large things and small (the automobile, the "Motown Sound," corn flakes, and baby food to cite a few examples).

We also saw a full-color self-portrait that included some of the most beautiful beaches in the world, bright blue lakes that stretch to the horizon, true wilderness where wolves and moose roam free, the largest pleasure boat fleet in America, world-class events such as the Detroit Grand Prix and the Montreux Detroit Jazz Festival, one of the oldest and most highly regarded state university systems in the United States. And the list goes on.

This book is that portrait, capturing some of the great moments—and some of the little moments—of that 150th year. It illustrates some timeless moments from Michigan's past and captures what Catton called "a place where the past, the present, and the future are all tied up in a hard knot . . . the skyscraper, the mass production line . . . golden sand, blue water (and) green pine trees on empty hills . . ."

We learned a lot about ourselves when we stopped to take this look. We hope you will pause, take a look, see what we saw, and learn what we learned.

A Portrait of Michigan at One Hundred Fifty

W inter struggles with spring and inevitably loses. Seemingly fragile blossoms shake off the last of the ice and snow and once again transform Michigan into one of America's most beautiful and productive gardens. Trees blossom on the State Capitol grounds and gardeners have made Detroit's Eastern Market Flower Day so popular that two of them are held each spring.

The Great Lakes have made Michigan a multi-million-acre orchard, producing much of America's supply of cherries, apples, plums, and peaches. There is perhaps no better way to grasp the size and the beauty of this industry than to fly over it on a soft spring morning.

The same generous gifts of nature—the fertile soil, the lake-tempered climate, the gentle, rolling hills, the long, lingering seasons—produce another incredible crop: more public golf courses than in any other state. Some with such quality "designer" labels as Jack Nicklaus and Arnold Palmer.

7

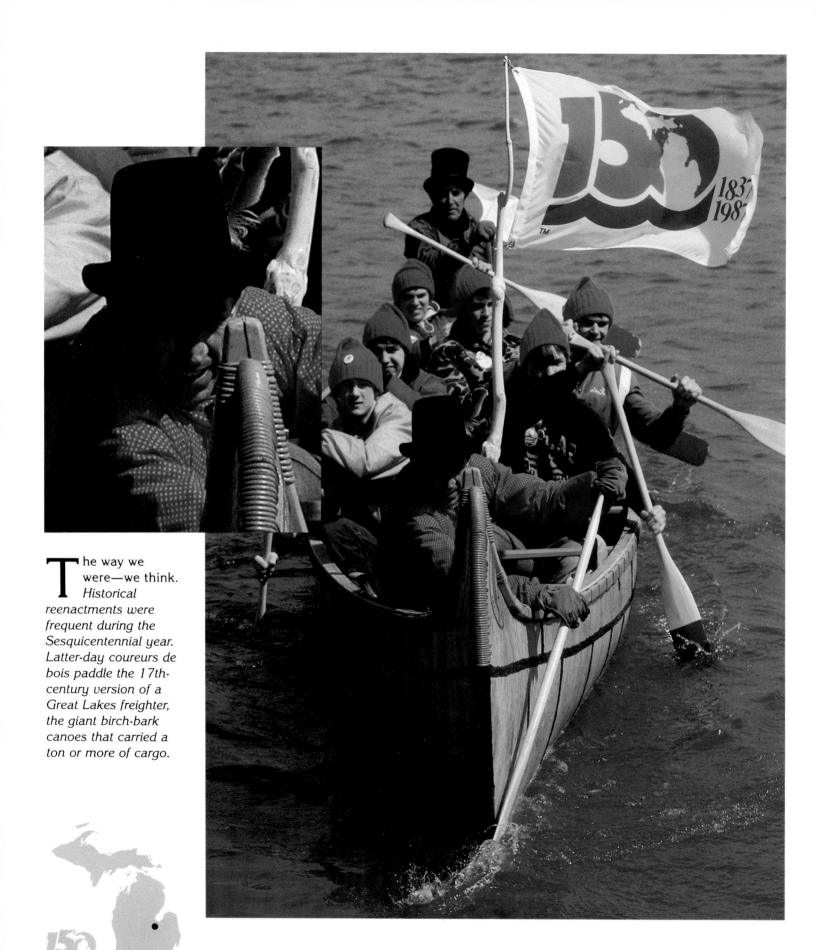

The way we were—we think. *Historical reenactments were frequent during the Sesquicentennial year. Latter-day coureurs de bois paddle the 17th-century version of a Great Lakes freighter, the giant birch-bark canoes that carried a ton or more of cargo.*

10

The way we are. *One spring day, an Amtrak special cruised across lower Michigan from Chicago to Detroit. The Sesquicentennial Whistlestop Train carried Michigan dignitaries (including Tony the Tiger and the Sesqui-Bear) to communities all along the route. Michiganians meeting other Michiganians.*

The way we've always been. Sleeping Bear Dunes National Lakeshore is one of Michigan's greatest, largest, and most intriguing landmarks. At 450-500 feet, the largest freshwater dunes in the world date back to the time when the glaciers dumped huge deposits of sand on the edge of what would one day be Lake Michigan.

The way we'll always be. *Isle Royale—a "new" island (only about 11,000 years old) built on rock billions of years old was a mining site some 4,000 years ago. Today, preserved by nature, it is a rugged emerald island protected by the frigid, blue waters of Lake Superior and home to moose and wolves.*

*W*ith nearly 19 million acres (more than half the state) still forested, with more than 36,000 miles of rivers and streams and 11,000 inland lakes, and with its strategic location as a migratory way-station, Michigan is home to an incredible variety of birds—from the Canada Goose to the Robin, the state bird.

Taking a cue from the birds, growing numbers of Michiganians are taking up the sport of hot-air ballooning and Battle Creek has hosted national and international balloon races. The sport has grown so much that the Department of Natural Resources has actually built a "balloonport" in one of its southeastern Michigan state parks.

An Arizona newspaper reports: "The western shores of Lake Michigan are far superior to the shorelines in San Diego and Los Angeles." Great praise coming from the heart of the "Sunbelt." Here, a solitary couple seems to have the entire 300-mile Lake Michigan shoreline to itself, while frolicking children enjoy a small stretch of Michigan's 3200-mile coastline.

23

The coastline is not all soft, sandy beaches either. Sometimes the lake scene shifts from beautiful to spectacular. Lake Superior has carved caves and coves and "castles" into a 35-mile-long stretch of multicolored sandstone cliffs—now preserved as Pictured Rocks National Lakeshore.

Once a fishing village, always a fishing village. Charming Leland has had a life as a commercial fishing village, an artists' colony, a sailors' haven, and a tourist attraction. It still has. Today, commercial fishing operations share the waters of the Great Lakes with charter boats, while Leland shares its fisherman's wharf with tourists and artists.

F rom the Great Lakes to the Grand Prix: some of Michigan's thrills are quiet and almost personal. Say, the struggle between a man or woman and a 20-pound salmon. Others are noisy and gregarious. For example, the Grand Prix, where the roar of Formula One engines and the babel of foreign languages fill the streets of downtown Detroit (or d'Étroit, to get back to the original French).

G rand! Grand! Grand! Grand Prix. Grand Traverse. Grand River. Grand Rapids. Grand Haven. Grand Island. Are all these "grands" warranted in one state? Well, these scenes of the Grand Hotel on Mackinac Island, taken during its centennial year, may answer the question.

And even when Mackinac Island, home of the Grand Hotel, isn't "grand," it is pleasant and unique. Unique in what way? To begin with, no cars. And, look, not a fast food restaurant in sight.

33

I ndependence Day is always important and special, but in 1987 the celebration took on special meaning. Bay City produced its traditional massive fireworks display. And Escanaba staged a special parade to salute the men and women who fought and died in Vietnam.

In Escanaba's Vietnam Veterans' Parade, an old soldier, a survivor of "the War to End All Wars" stood proud, honoring those who fought in America's "last" war. Meanwhile, the 1st Michigan Colonial Fife and Drum Corps paraded at Detroit's historic Fort Wayne.

O ur future meets our past. Long before Michigan put the world on wheels, wheels helped bring the world to Michigan—in covered wagons. A young Michiganian, who will spend his entire adult life in the 21st century, gets a taste of the 19th in the Sesquicentennial Wagon Train.

*J*ust a few of the more than 700,000 pleasure boats registered in Michigan: the largest pleasure boat fleet in America.

There are times when it is best to say nothing and let the scene speak for itself. The scene: Silver Lake Dunes State Park in the background, Silver Lake in the foreground.

National Governors' Associat

79th ANNUAL MEETING

GOVERNOR DUKAKIS Massachusetts

GOVERNOR HARRIS Georgia

...TIN Carolina

The New York Times *has called the Traverse City region "a place where important people meet to exchange ideas and do important things." The nation's governors and Chrysler Chairman Lee Iacocca met, exchanged ideas, and discussed America's role in the world economy during the Annual Meeting of the National Governors' Association.*

Great issues in the morning; great times in the evening. The governors and their guests capped a long day of meetings with a long midsummer evening of festivities on the lawn of Grand Traverse Resort Village. The food at this all-Michigan picnic ranged from plain to fancy, and the music ranged from J. C. Heard's Orchestra to the 126th Army National Guard Band.

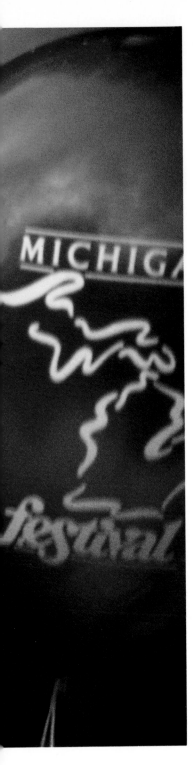

This could be the start of something big! *And it was. The spirit of the Michigan Sesquicentennial was guaranteed a life beyond 1987 with the immensely popular first annual Michigan Festival—a celebration of Michigan folklore and arts and crafts on the campus of Michigan State University. Folk singer Josh White Jr., was one of the scores of Michigan-connected entertainers at the ten-day festival.*

etroit is a festival almost every day: Whether it's the crowds on the streets of Greektown every weekend, the crowds in historic Trappers Alley almost any time, or an angler alone with his pole and his thoughts on Detroit's Belle Isle as the setting sun puts the city in perspective a few miles downstream.

*M*ichigan's cities are nice places to visit—and you would want to live there. In addition, regardless of their size they have had an impact on America and the world. *Grand Rapids (left) was the home of President Gerald R. Ford. and is the home of the Gerald Ford Museum. Battle Creek (below) changed the way the world eats breakfast. And Flint (lower left) changed the lives of working men and women forever.*

Another look at the unchanging Michigan. This particular stretch of Lake Huron probably looked like this 10,000 years ago. And, if we are conscientious stewards of our great natural resources, it will look like this 10,000 years from now.

It's one of Michigan's mystic places; people speak of it with a certain awe. Those who have seen it seem to share a certain fellowship. And yet, it is easily accessible. A long drive and a short walk down an easy woodland path and suddenly you are on an escarpment looking down on the Porcupine Mountains' Lake of the Clouds.

Someone once said that Michigan is where autumn comes home. Here it lingers long and stays late. Autumn is nature's highway beautification program—Michigan style.

Michigan has always been on the cutting edge of social issues. It was not surprising, then, that Pope John Paul II visited Detroit in September to deliver a major address on social problems and to visit one of America's largest Polish communities. Tens of thousands turned out for his mass in the Silverdome sports stadium and on the streets of Hamtramck, a Polish enclave in Detroit.

L eave it to Detroit to do what everybody else does—but with a twist. The Detroit Free Press Marathon, for example, starts in Canada, crosses an international bridge, circles an island, and ends up in the center of the city. And, it is open to all who care to compete.

*M*ichigan was populated in large measure by settlers from New England and upstate New York. It is no accident, then, that many of Michigan's autumn scenes create a certain sense of deja vu.

In summer, fall, winter, and spring, millions of Michiganians had something to celebrate. In college football, Michigan State University emerged Big Ten and Rose Bowl champs, while the University of Michigan was victorious in the Hall of Fame Bowl and Eastern Michigan University triumphed in the California Bowl.

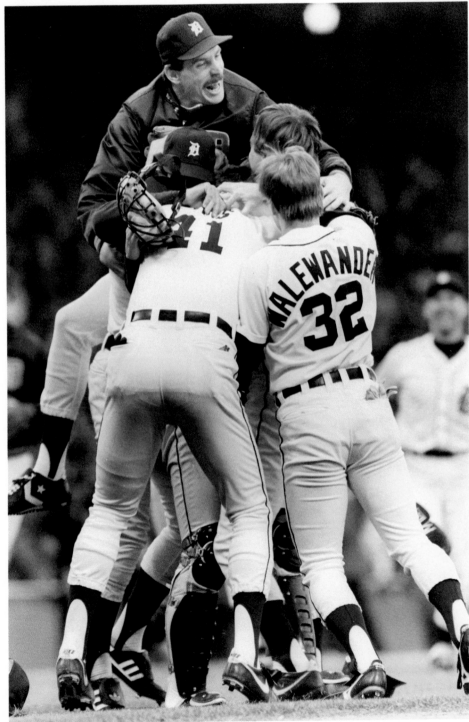

The Detroit Tigers climbed to the top of the American League East, while the Detroit Pistons and Red Wings reminded the world that Detroit is a sports power to be reckoned with year-round.

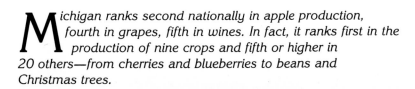

Michigan ranks second nationally in apple production, fourth in grapes, fifth in wines. In fact, it ranks first in the production of nine crops and fifth or higher in 20 others—from cherries and blueberries to beans and Christmas trees.

The rapids of the St. Marys River (or Sault Ste. Marie in the original French) serve as the lone outlet for the world's largest freshwater lake. Here, the 2,900 cubic miles of water in Lake Superior tumble 21 feet over the rocks into the lower Great Lakes. Thousand-foot freighters bypass those rapids through some of the largest locks in the world: the Soo Locks.

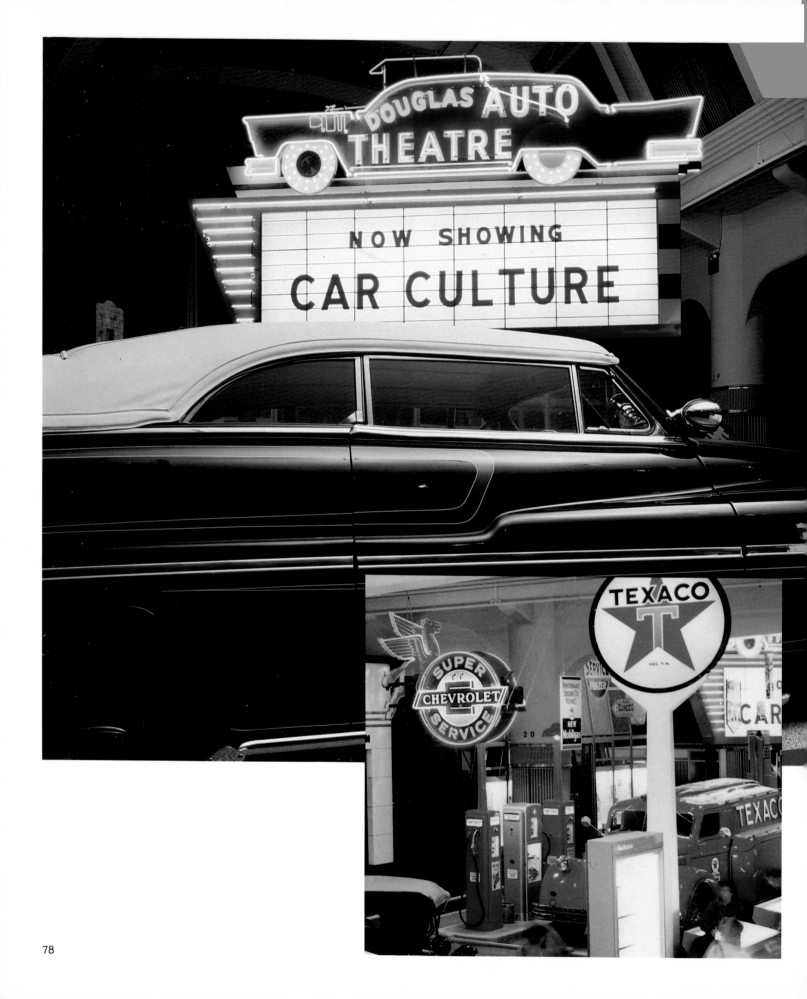

W here else could a customized 1949 Mercury coexist with the early 19th-century architecture of Martha Mary Chapel but at Henry Ford Museum & Greenfield Village? Here, the world's largest collection of 19th-century Americana meets the world's first museum exhibit to explore the impact of the automobile on 20th-century America: "The Automobile in American Life."

We have found so many ways to turn the clear, crisp days and deep, white snows of winter to our advantage that sometimes the season seems all too short. How do we do it? Let us count the ways: skiing (downhill and cross-country—such as in the North American VASA race pictured here), skating, snowmobiling, fishing, sledding, ballooning, and even winter golf.

W inter can transform beautiful sights into glorious attractions. Proof of that statement is Tahquamenon Falls, one of the largest waterfalls east of the Mississippi. With its copper-colored waters, it has been famous since it was immortalized in Longfellow's Song of Hiawatha.

With nearly 50 ski resorts, thousands of miles of cross-country trails, the highest elevations between the Alleghenies and the Black Hills, and the most consistent snowfall in the region (a gift from the surrounding Great Lakes), Michigan is the ski capital of the Midwest.

W hen Santa Claus comes to <u>this</u> town, Detroit, they greet him with one of the largest and oldest parades in America, The Michigan Thanksgiving Parade, and the key to the city. Detroit Mayor Coleman A. Young does the honors, while another Detroit "mover"—the new People Mover, passes overhead.

In December the glitter of a Christmas tree replaced the glow of the blossoming trees on the Capitol lawn. In the meantime, the Sesquicentennial presented the opportunity for Michigan to return the 108-year-old Capitol building to its former splendor.

An already completed $1 million restoration is only part of a massive program to assure Michiganians that by the time they reach the 21st century, they will again enjoy what they had in 1879: a working capitol with elegant style and appointments.

Michigan's Sesquicentennial Christmas tree (at 75 feet, the largest ever and taller than the one in Rockefeller Center) was lighted in front of the State Capitol by Governor James Blanchard— with a little help from some young friends.

The ghosts of Christmases past seem to stare out of the windows of Fayette, Michigan's best-known ghost town, where the seasons are the only changes you will see, and where 1987 was just another in a long chain of years.

The year winds down. And like a perfect winter day, the celebration ends softly in a golden glow that promises a bright future.

14/15 ●

Lake Superior

60/61 ●
16/17

42/43 ●

24/25 ● 16

82/83 ●

76/77 ●

84/85 ●

62/63 ●

34/35 ●
80/81

90/91 ●

30/33 ●

58/59 ●

70/71 ●

27 ●

Lake Huron

26 ● 39 ●

12/13 ●
44/45 ● 6/7
74 ●
46/49 ● 81

84 ●

Michigan touches on four of the five Great Lakes, giving it a 3200-mile coastline—longer than the entire Atlantic seaboard of the United States.

Some 40,000 square miles of Great Lakes waters lie within Michigan's borders. It is not surprising, therefore, that 700,000 pleasure boats are registered here—the largest pleasure boat fleet in America.

Lake Michigan

40/41 ●
42 ●

23 ●

8/9 ●

54 ●

20/21 ●
55 ● 11

4/5 ●

22/23 ●

56/57 ●

68/69 ● 10 ●
34/35 ●

54 ●

72 ●
2 ● 50/51
88/89 ● 36/37

92/93 ● 7 ●
64/65 ● 38/39
72 ● 52/53
66/67 ● 3
78/79 ● 28/29
73 ● 86/87
75 ● 86

Lake Erie

A Portrait of Michigan at One Hundred Fifty

Some of Michigan's best photographers have contributed to this publication. However, fully one-third of the photos displayed here are the work of a man whose images have shaped the world's view of Michigan for nearly 20 years. Although Gilbert N. Clarke, staff photographer for the Michigan Travel Bureau, 1968-1986, passed away on the eve of the Sesquicentennial Year, the world will continue to see Michigan through his eyes for years to come.

The photographs in this book were provided by the following photographers and organizations:

Cover Photo:
South Manitou Island Lighthouse
Gil Clarke

Back Cover Photo:
Mackinac Bridge
Jim Karas

Page No.	Photo Credit
1	Sunrise **Gil Clarke** **Michigan Travel Bureau**
2	Capitol Building **Gil Clarke**
	Blossoms **Gil Clarke**
3	Flower Day **Balthazar Korab**
4/5	Orchard Aerial **Gil Clarke**
6/7	Golfers **Balthazar Korab**
7	Golfers and Blossoms **Gil Clarke**
8	Holland **Holland Color Camera Club**
	Tulips **Felicia Preston**
9	Children's Parade **Holland Color Camera Club**
10	Voyageurs **Dick Van Nostrand** **Bay City Times**
11	Whistlestop Tour **Michigan Department of Transportation**
12/13	Sleeping Bear Dunes **Gil Clarke**
14	Isle Royale Moose **John and Ann Mahan**
14/15	Isle Royale **Stan Osolinski**
16	Wagner Falls **Gil Clarke**

Page No.	Photo Credit
16/17	Shining Cloud Falls **Dan Urbanski**
18/19	Canada Geese **Gil Clarke**
19	Robin **Gil Clarke**
20/21	Balloons **Gil Clarke**
22/23	Warren Dunes State Park **Balthazar Korab**
23	Children on Beach **Gil Clarke**
24/25	Pictured Rocks National Lakeshore **Abrams Aerial Survey Corporation**
26/27	Leland Harbor **Gil Clarke**
27	Charter Boat **Gil Clarke**
28	Grand Prix Driver **Robert Brodbeck** **AAA Michigan**
	Grand Prix Crowd **Detroit Renaissance Grand Prix Inc.**
29	Grand Prix Driver **Robert Brodbeck** **AAA Michigan**
30	Grand Hotel Porch **Jim Karas** **Michigan Travel Bureau**
	Grand Hotel **Balthazar Korab**

Page No.	Photo Credit
31	Grand Hotel Lawn **Balthazar Korab**
32/33	Mackinac Island Main Street **Gil Clarke**
33	Mackinac Island **Jim Karas**
34	Fireworks **Dick Van Nostrand** **Bay City Times**
	Veterans **Tom Buchkoe**
35	Fife and Drum Corps **Robert Brodbeck** **AAA Michigan**
	World War I Soldier **Tom Buchkoe**
36/37	Wagon Train **George Waldman** **Detroit Free Press**
37	Cowboy **Manny Chrisostomo** **Detroit Free Press**
38/39	Marina **Gil Clarke**
39	Sailboat **Balthazar Korab**
40/41	Silver Lake Dunes **John Penrod**
42	Lighthouse **Gil Clarke**
42/43	Lighthouse **Gil Clarke**

MORE . . .